Categorics

Categorics
1, 2 & 3

Normand de Bellefeuille

Translated by D.G. Jones

Coach House Press

Toronto

Published with the assistance of the Canada Council, the Ontario
Arts Council and the Department of Communications.

Canadian Cataloguing in Publication Data

Bellefeuille, Normand de, 1949–
    [Catégoriques. English]
    Categorics: one two and three

Poems.
Translation of: Catégoriques.
ISBN 0-88910-452-2

I. Title. II. Title: Catégoriques. English.

PS8553.E4576C3713 1992   C841'.54   C92-095509-6
PQ3919.2.B45C3713 1992

For Monique Grandmangin, my Ariadne
amid the maze of French syntax
and semantic turns.

D.G.J.

what's the point of writing to say
exactly what one had to say?
Cioran

one can't say everything
Vincent Descombes

"Categorics"

The predicate. The family. Sometimes the shambles.

But there is also the question of voice, the gestures, the rhythms, whose precise implications we argue, or of signs, to put it simply, whose secret number is a matter of dispute, even — never mind the Gnostics — in the three mixed shades. Aristotle. Kant. Nietzsche. The concept. The shambles. Sometimes the whole sentence: ideology, but without much weight.

It's in a higher sense, higher in our "desire for the worst," that the figure gets worked out, barely, that the noise takes shape, word for word, step by step, in a higher sense, in our "desire for the worst": historical irony at grips with so many categories of thought, beauty and her train, but also the quotidian, the idiotic quotidian.

I

TIME

for Louise Dupré

Without music, life would be a mistake.

Nietzsche

I While Listening to Philip Glass

Music that admittedly makes noise is at the same time the improbable occasion of our own silence. Music is consternation.

To enter you while listening to Philip Glass; here in this cozy shelter you make up for my modern blues and the real is really close, all the more as it swoons, yes, as it slides away from one's mouth and slips from under the hand that insists. Then you'd think we were back in history class, passing the answers between two desks, overly varnished, as you whisper: "tell me, do you still believe in progress?" The rough sheet, listening to Philip Glass, and the wild remedy that reminds us that death, after all, leaves much of the body, that death, not to put too fine a point on it, doesn't finish the job. And it is that, certainly, listening to Philip Glass, the unthinkable drama of not being, each time not radical enough, each time hedging just a little, regretting almost the organs that it throws out and takes back, that each time it spits out and sucks in, that it neglects and retains, each time hardly long enough to remember or to call a bad scene.

Gently you reset the needle, Einstein, Akhenaton or Ghandi, I'm no longer sure, but I think he is happy that music that admittedly makes noise may also be the improbable occasion of our own silence. You smile, rest your head there, and pull up the sheet. And my desire is consternation.

2 A Song for the Coming War

You imagine, you say, out of the blue, that it's me, this time, who is playing. The instrument as you picture it to yourself — and how, at this hour, could it be otherwise — is primitive, without strings or pipes, yet stuns, clangs and clacks, precipitates, note by note, a song for the coming war, with its cries, its moans, with its raucous and its barbarous notes, a song for the coming war that ought to, you think, be called **Fin de siècle: Venice and New York;** you repeat, a little too solemnly, the title: **Fin de siècle: Venice and New York,** and you make up the innumerable words, articulating them one by one in an exaggerated manner, though I can only catch "hip," "dance," "angle" and, perhaps equally, "sea," "bedroom," "mouth," such words, so much does the instrument, without strings, without pipes, clang and clack, precipitate a song for the coming war: **Fin de siècle: Venice and New York.**

Now you sing, imagining it's me, this time, who is playing, imagining also the stage, without sets, but deeper than canyons, ruins, or dizzying fjords, you imagine the trap and the pit where the sounds emerge, imagine the vault, the close, the last mile, imagine the canvas that falls, white and yellow, **white and yellow with its curtained flowers.**

Fin de siècle: Venice and New York, a song for the coming war, with its raucous and its barbarous notes.

3 Indifference, Murmur

The site of a certain prehistory. Luxuriously oceanic the "there is" of a certain prehistory. Less a matter of memory (Theory of Capital, Solfeggio) than of forgetting, less in the rehearsal itself — breathy noises, throaty noises, nasal noises — less a matter of the accumulation of sense or emotions than of their loss (Theory of Improvidence!): riffs and drones, a cough and its croup, but altogether an operatic diction springing from a fabulous body wholly head and torso, the luxuriously oceanic "there is" of a certain prehistory; counter-music, this cough and its croup, irrevocably, to the point of secret amnesia.

It exists only as a revenant which strays and meanders, which braces itself before the catastrophe and, in its supreme indifference, murmurs: "we are so little prepared for repetition." It composes noise, what strays and meanders and only exists as a revenant, composes the ambient noise, distinguishing and prolonging each note to the point of absence, convinced then that **even after its death, there will be sounds.**

"We are so little prepared for repetition"; elsewhere the tenor, always the same tenor, generously spreads his arse and prepares his cry.

4 Bands in the Bedroom

Let's imagine the blinds, loosed, clattering down, the flags as well and the hats that roll about with a lot of noise. Let's imagine the children gone wild and the bands in the shells of damp cupboards. The play begins.

Let's imagine all the machinery and the springs that creak under the bed and lie in wait for the crook of the elbow, or worse still the neck that nonchalantly sometimes strays outside the perimeter, imprudently adventures to the extreme limit of the sheet the better to hear the racket below: all the machinery and the springs that creak, clearly there are creatures in the bedroom; let's imagine them, then, their trumpeting sex composing an orchestra.

For there exists, it's obvious, a music proper to childhood, that pounds out rhythms when the heart is already too small for the blood, when the blinds come clattering down, the flags as well and the hats that roll about with a lot of noise, and that evokes, with so much precision, now the hundreds of mouths in the rusty troughs, now the ridiculous craving for lemonade. There exists a music proper to childhood, which comes to life on those oppressive evenings when the night lights one two and three flicker yellow and black and flare in the bedrooms that mothers have shut up too early; since clearly there are creatures in the room. Who play. Who whisper. Who pound. Who start up again, and again, right through to morning, when at last one can read the light, silent on the boulevards.

5 As Close as You Can Get Perhaps to Silence

For I mean "reading" above the disorder: the trembling at times in the dressing gowns of the family, rising, when it spreads to areas perhaps as close as you can get to silence, the quivering in the dressing gowns over and above the disorder since none has really written, none has really read who hasn't already, with the cane and the sound, looked on as bit by bit the admirable scene unfolds: a certain theory of the sentence, a certain theory of the sentence including even its derailment, including even its harmony and even its counter-harmony above the disorder, sometimes the air, **so slight, of Vinteuil as the national anthem of their love,** sometimes of Monteverdi, above all of **Vespers,** above all of echo, sometimes, much more simply, dramatic or casual, the noise of the book that, impatient and dry, cracks open in its very spine!

"Reading" still, choosing one's yarns, with a delicate pursing of the lips, without too much thought about the knots and the bows, neither, however, making it a mystery, behind, against the wall, melody doubly concealed, this unavoidable necessity of the knots and the bows; thus, all the same, one must write: "there are, it's astonishing, vowels with the deepest thoughts and cries unique to every opera."

Above the disorder, a certain theory of the sentence, with its knots and its bows behind it, with certain vowels and certain cries when perhaps especially it spreads to areas as close as you can get to silence, a certain theory of the sentence that defies the scene even as it crosses it, that defies the song that tirelessly, rising above the disorder and never, for all that, adding to it, it repeats.

6 While Listening to John Cage

That's pretty well how, that day, we had to write; pretty well making, that day, beyond language, all the noise we had to: writing as friction — the rustling of organs: sighs, rattles — and of motors, friction — of organs: sighs, rattles — and astonishing whistles. For after the noise, tied to the mast or, turned to the sea, and stuck in our teeth still all the names of the other-worlds, there were, precisely between the sense and the music, voices to which one could scarcely attach faces, tied to the mast or, turned to the sea, and stuck in our teeth still all the names of the other-worlds, there were voices one assumed to be understood, **sous-entendues,** but of which one said, this time, truly, **"we had to state the sous-entendues, beyond language, that day, amid the racket, the body's anxieties when, after the noise, it goes on loving without understanding, carried away without understanding, at last, exactly, while listening: friction — of organs: sighs, rattles — and of motors, friction — of organs: sighs, rattles — and astonishing whistles."**

That's pretty well how, that day, we had to write: not so much out of passion as, in the profusion, the actions made flesh, not so much out of passion as out of the luxuriance of passion: to enter you while listening to John Cage, convinced, yet again, that form liberates, that form renews.

Otherwise, how could things have been as they were? How could you have known, already smiling, to murmur, "remember now the end of the world, remember forever this morning!"

7 The Occident of Things

Here it is: mortal, beyond consolation, we flinched beneath the sky and its thousands of skinny birds.

I thought I could recognize in this, unpronounceable, deliciously unpronounceable, the joy and the gravity of a very ancient musical motif. The question would be, and still is, the risks of navigation and of the trees, slightly naked, with leaves only on the left, with only on the left, like so many outdated instruments, the laughter and the song of their upturned leaves. So, beyond consolation, we flinched beneath the sky and its thousands of skinny birds.

Still, in the same tonalities, as far as possible from any melody you might figure out, the sea one can't forget — deny, just like that, its depth, and you recall irrevocably the code (Theory of Coupling!) — the sea with its waves only on the left, with only on the left — should one say the bodice of some outmoded dresses? — one two and three the laughter and the song of the astonished beasts. The trees without method. The sea without method. There where matter, without worrying about filling a vacuum or, for that matter, without denying either History or the World, becomes itself, finally, with its knots and its bows, theatrical, affirmative. The trees without method. The sea without method; it's the occident of things.

8 Concerning Song, the Lips Rather

We need to find another activity than art: we are leaving
for China. We hope our visit will leave no trace.

John Cage

But when the voices in the garden are silenced will we find
even oblivion?

Evoke: first concerning the garden, all the nuances and the
paths carefully marked, then concerning the song, the lips
rather, which you may well imagine — let's suppose that they
are well limned and the breath is lightly sketched if one keeps
track of the solemn tune they interpret — or equally, in the
refrain, the stresses of emotion, comparable each time to the
slow and oblique progression of the heavy continental plates:
for the object of the World — its prose! — is hardly much dif-
ferent, there, at its deepest, in the beginning of speech, in the
ordinary business of dying: a music endlessly confronting the
noise that always, however, returns and that happily, like the
organ grinder, has no name in any speech. Does not, then, the
most exact operation consist in clearing up the entire world, in
repeating, against the illegitimacy of the cry, the sounds of
these immense spaces?

Not to be anymore blind to the real, not anymore to miss the
real: allowing the landscape and the Atlantic to return, allow-
ing the murmurings, the heart and the draughtsmen of
Lascaux to return, colouring, if you will, the atlases and, each
time it rains, the underside of my fingernails, ekindling the
fire and rekindling the fire the moment it's gone out, not to be
blind to the real, allowing the real to return when the voices in
the garden are silenced: there in the beginning of speech, in
the ordinary business of dying.

9 Mortal, I Had a Voice

if something bores you after
two minutes, try four
Oriental Saying

I think as a mortal, I listen in the same way. I listen as a mortal. In terms, of course, of my own death, but even more perhaps in terms of the sound that the moment — indeed the moment's breath — carelessly wipes out. But this sound is **not missed,** is not **missing.** For definitely nowhere else is there — even in its absence! — such an awareness of enduring. Each sound is an irreducible and strict comment on duration.

And even though it **never celebrates any other mystery than that,** there are no boring sounds; each ensures us measureless encounters; islands without geographers, a precise landscape, forgotten summers with loose dresses revealing breasts (yellow, perhaps, the dresses, and small, perhaps, the breasts).

I think as a mortal. I listen in the same way. There often follow certain joys, felicities very close to the poem, very close to the unknowable echoes within the damp tunnels of childhood: I was a child; mortal, I had a voice.

I0 The Precise Index of Emotion

At each moment and forever, repeated like aphorisms, those that every morning in a few quick phrases (mimetic at first, then idiosyncratically narrative) usher in the whole of Nature; those that while so similar to the line similar to the other line thus assuring the eternal return demonstrate decisively that there is never really a return of the **Same;** those that patiently label, establish, decree, and affect "the voice of the father," "the voice of totality"; others, as well, delightfully "off," **fine-tuned** one might say by the very breath of suffering, the very breath of pleasure, the very rhythms or fevers more rare than Melody or the precise Index of emotion; and, finally, those rising in the euphoria of repetition and which one might characterize as "made up" with the help of certain giant powder boxes, poetically precious in the assiduity of their art and in permitting us to hear, **at the pitch of death,** only their voices, the strongest, most foreign and shrouded to History; **at the pitch of death** they rise up only to fall silent after having sung but once; for those are self-consuming, make no sense except as thoughts-between-worlds.

At each moment and for ever, repeated like aphorisms, as in a mirror one reads the blotters used on notebooks, as one makes out, all at once, an image in the wallpaper: with hesitations, with impatience, sometimes with irritation or anger even — with the painful pleasure of walking on naked bodies of women with their supplicating arms.

All that precisely at the limit of **hearing,** and of **not hearing,** all that like delving in the void, not less mute fine-tuned one might say by the very breath of pleasure, the very breath of suffering, the very fevers or rhythms more rare than Melody or the precise Index of emotion.

II While Listening to Liz Story

You listen. It's odd but, as if you were talking, **you insist** while listening. Happy in the bath, you listen with a gin in hand, quiet, but insistent. The pianist is called Liz Story. There's a piece entitled "Things With Wings," another entitled "Solid Colours." The pianist's name sets you dreaming. It's a woman's story and you listen.

There are words, you say, which you can no longer bear to read, to hear: "desire," "body," "Montreal," **"What I'd really like right now is for us to visit a volcano, and China ... above all, I don't want to hear another word about the desert!"** You take the bottle and pour, hardly disturbing a limb under the water. And methodically, you drink. And this time you mutter, barely audible, muffled by the elegant glass you still press firmly to your lips: **"I'm relieved, so relieved, to no longer have a soul."**

You make up words to go with these slow tunes. It's often a matter of **leaves, sea with brown algae, women alone in narrow rooms.** You sing, imagining that it's me who plays, imagining as well the stage, without sets, but deeper still than canyons, ruins, or dizzying fjords. You finish your gin, you smile, and slip, silently, completely disappearing, under the water, while I, standing, and fully attired, applaud.

12 Each Cry Its Particular Light

For to say that the cry goes back to our origins in no way attenuates the terrible presence of the cry. The cry of the city, the cry of the forest. Each cry has its zone. The cry of the docks, the cry of the marshalling yards, of the lakeshore, quite unlike the cry of the caravan, the muffled cry of the vein, the sharp cry of the sword in the vein; each cry has its zone, and each its particular light: some on their knees in the fervent dark, others stopped precisely at the level of young breasts (first love!), some whose tone is muted by History, the timbre as much as the interminable echo: each cry has its zone and each its given name, let's retain, for the moment, only Jeanne and Olivier, let's orchestrate, let's orchestrate these cries!

Each is a **revenant,** hot blood in its jaws nourishing the hollow space within, a voice sombre and thin (effigy, figurine!), cannon at the cannon's mouth, it is the negation of itself. Let's orchestrate these cries. Each escapes at the high point, the high point of the thighs — where the legs join — where it lets go with a voice sombre and thin (effigy, figurine!), and sprays milt on the hem of the void.

To say that the cry goes back to our origins in no way attenuates the terrible presence of the cry. The cry of the old world wounded or of heavy stuffs where the cry, cloaked, turns back on itself. The interminable cry, never repeated, of pleasure. The cry. So many cries. Against evil and madness.

13 Certain Noises are Sevenths

There is surely a "false note," one, at the end of
Phédon, as there is in the **Socrate** by Satie,
the jar of C natural against C sharp.
Vladimir Jankélévitch

A happenstance, and a happy one: the slight disorder of sevenths in the Rules of Harmony. As well, there are pretty catastrophes, certain noises of this kind are sevenths: the tea one pours, the fans that almost touch, a small boat on the wide river, a heart that knocks; look no further, certainly look no further, there is no mystery to unveil, nothing except the universe: the last round before mourning; look no further, the horror is real.

There are, believe me, various versions of this pain you have in your breast, which rises in the throat right to your teeth; amid the general noise, radiating out, various versions of your own disappearance. You would wish it, of course, prodigious, one of the rare slight disorders — an unpublished seventh! — in the Rules of Harmony, you would wish it sovereign and minor at the same time the tea that one pours a small boat on the wide river, but it remains beyond science, beyond strategy, beyond science or felicitous dissonance: the horror is real, yes, eurythmic and grave that good product, your death, this pain still that you have in your breast.

Socrates takes the bowl. Having loved and nothing more. Socrates takes the bowl, as in the canvas by David, the hands of the hangman (does one always say hands even if he never touches the victim?). The slight disorder of the sevenths, a happenstance, and a happy one, in the Rules of Harmony. Having loved and nothing more.

14 This Music in a Field of Shallots

She exaggerates Venice!
Claude Haeffely

Haven't we imagined it, you and I, the carnival of Babylon (a whole morning off, and somehow Italian, on the unimaginable lagoons of Babel), and then, equally, a whole continent away that of Brazil with Argentinian tunes, with steps that one two and three never cease to begin the beguine, to awaken the body, to reawaken its joy. At this moment I say, **"Once — it was almost Easter, I remember the saints in their purple shrouds, all that week, I remember the acquiescent angels — I ate éclairs in the odour of permanents, and equally I kept foul memories of the drugstore-yellowing hair,"** but I know the most important thing's to be able to murmur, later: **"Haven't we imagined, you and I, the carnival of Babylon, and, then, a whole continent away, that of Brazil with Argentinian tunes?"**

This music in the courtyards, this music in the corridors, and hummed, barely, in long sculls, or else, naked, large thighs in a field of shallots; this music has nothing to do with the obscure and unpractisable virtues, this music in the courtyards, this music in the cloudy corridors of houses with towers and warm window panes never ceases to awaken the body, to reawaken its joy.

That's the hardest truth of all, that it exists in every fiction — Venice, Lascaux, Babylon — an unending memory of the first festival, a memory that condemns us, masked, to slowly repeating the tunes in the long sculls or in the cloudy corridors of houses with towers.

I5 Geryon's Concert

The problem with the cry is
its widespread banality.
Robert Hébert

It sometimes happens that noise clarifies, exposes; it happens that the cry reveals what the rigged text otherwise invites us to read (for example, Hercules and his low concert of Geryon's cattle), what the text with its complex curves — its contradictions — duplicitously, already implied: well, this time the meaning truly **comes out** of the cave, for it happens that it becomes precisely noised about, for it happens that noise clarifies, exposes the ruse of the reversed hoofprints of Geryon's cattle.

It is, then, precisely when it withdraws that the cry, like a slap in the face, like a slap in the face, hails us, in the heat of the moment that welds lightness and intimate recognition. Do we know how to think this cry, assumed from the beginning, which thunders the darkness of sense — since it **comes out,** this time from the cave — impenetrable and barred up to then? Can we, calmly, take the millennia necessary to understand it, like a slap, like a slap, the chiaroscuro and the slow unfolding (the same knot undone thread by thread, the same knot re-tied thread by thread)?

For example, Hercules and the low concert of Geryon's cattle: before History, the truth, without shadows, inarticulate — this **mad** noise that one nonethless said was **primal, from the depths** — that **comes out** of the cave, that clarifies and exposes the reversed hoofprints.

16 Against the Fourteen Strains of Melancholy

Music is sometimes credible, for example when the pianist is called Liz Story. The same goes for reality — the blood and its whirlwinds; a nearly tropical landscape. A little sacrifice, a little murder, a weapon in fact and an oath, music is credible and effective against the fourteen strains of melancholy. Of course, this is not accomplished without noise (think of the animals, the fish, the walls of Thebes!), this is certainly not accomplished without a crisis, a small **catastrophe;** we are no longer in the world of the eternal, but of the "never infinite," of the never to know, never to understand, never to hail (let alone say farewell to) the **onely** love. At this moment, heavy breathing and hands clapping, rather than the gratuitous radiance of the star or the flower in its perfect commotion. Music is credible, and effective against the fourteen strains of melancholy, but naturally that is not accomplished without noise, that certainly is not accomplished without a crisis, a small **catastrophe.**

So, only the real returns — the blood and its whirlwinds; a nearly tropical landscape. The real returns while dancing upon, while crying out that, the real returns even while talking ... think of the animals, the fish, the walls of Thebes, think of the water, the matted grass, the haying — while dancing upon, while crying out that ... even while talking about the things of the World.

Fourteen strains of melancholy. Against the fourteen strains of melancholy, heavy breathing and hands clapping, rather than the gratuitous radiance of the star or the flower in its perfect commotion.

I7 Dachau, in Slow Time or a Walking Beat

against noise, my noise
Henri Michaux

Take the Act of Vienna and the orchestras of Dachau.
Take the Act of Vienna and the orchestras of Dachau.
Take the Act of Vienna and the orchestras of Dachau.
Take the Act of Vienna and the orchestras of Dachau.
After that, who knows? At last maybe nine in the World, at
first to speak only to oneself — ideology, without weight!
— like an oyster, patiently fashioning its pearly depths, for
it's true that the form exists before giving itself to the
World, magnificent already before giving itself to the
World.

Take the Act of Vienna and the orchestras of Dachau. Your
eyelids — the colour of a dress! — flutter, quiet and deaf:
two insects plucked from the darkness, from the madness,
in slow time or a walking beat. Your eyelids, plucked from
the madness, display the number equal to the fatality of
Myth and the Future, against the snicker of Myth, against
the snicker of the Future; oh! you start the whole thing up
again, with each look, the whole cathedral!

This accomplishment performed amid a vague murmuring.
So far from Vienna and from Dachau. For it's true that the
form exists before giving itself to the World.

18 "Silence," as It Is Signalled in Music

I still haven't said enough, you think, about the **breakdown** — one almost needs a counter-writing in the gloom of the twilight — nor, you think, of the night that delivers us over to the night. However, isn't there a tune in every opening movement of thought — precisely at the point of writing, where the rhythm still rests in a swoon, in remission? But, you think, I still haven't said enough about the **breakdown** — for its depth isn't clear to me — nor yet, you think, of this tune, on the point of losing heart, in every opening movement of thought.

It seems to you that indeed there's some impediment in this world where one is able to write and that, on the subject of this impediment, I still have everything to say: the greatest luxury of poems, their silent ease (participating in silence/ "silence" as it is signalled in music: a brief **event** still when nothing takes place) and of the night that delivers us over to the night, infinitely returns us to the night!

I affirm nothing concerning the **breakdown,** above all I define nothing, neither the despair nor the bitter solitude that precedes it in every opening movement of thought. I affirm nothing except **the absence of any response,** except the night that delivers us over to the night.

19 Although He Says "I"

"Someone will have loved me the longest days of my life, will have lifted with a finger the certain convictions of the past, and lightly grazed, with a slow and indirect trace, my body and the river, someone will have allowed me, in the longest days of my life, to not reply, to reply, between speech and slumber, neither from my body nor from the river, will even have tried, in a neutral but accurate voice, a fundamental A, or la, on my ear, the perfect interval from A to my ear, someone will have raised me to a fever pitch the longest days of my life, but equally will have struck an ache, someone will suffer an intense ache in the final moment of my thought, which, on that particular night, tender and luminous, impassioned and luminous, could only be for her."

He speaks without precision, although he says "I," he speaks a defeated tongue, wildly outlandish, although he says "I," a tongue older than all history, he speaks without precision, but his love is a triumph, at the farthest remove from writing: "Someone will have loved me the longest days of my life." A clear world of faerie, each time, although he says "I"!

"I affirm nothing except the absence of any reply and this simple statement that death knocks on this particular night, tender and luminous: 'Do not overly regret writing, above all do not overly regret writing.' Lightly grazing with a slow and indirect trace my body and then the river, with the A, or la in my ear."

20 One Two and Three

"We are so little prepared for repetition." I think as a mortal, as one reads in mirrors the blotters of notebooks, as one hears the vowels, only the vowels sometimes, in the most profound thoughts. Midnight nearly. One two and three. Midnight nearly, midnight coloured by alcohol and by this writing which pounds out rhythms while the heart is already too small for the blood. Midnight nearly, in sevenths, all in sevenths, midnight nearly, and spring. Let's orchestrate these cries!

The inaudible even, one two and three, that sings fervently, sings extravagantly, beneath the so delicate and so transparent temples of the child you were, colouring your atlas and, each time it rained, the undersides of your fingernails. The inaudible even against the fourteen strains of melancholy of the child you were and that I would have loved. Nothing more. In this now nothing more than the sea without method and the night that infinitely returns us to the night. Midnight nearly, coloured by alcohol. Let's orchestrate this song for the coming war!

Will we know how to conceive this cry, turned to the sea, one two and three, turned to the sea, and stuck in our teeth still all the names of the other-worlds, will we know how to conceive this cry that death throws out and takes back, that each time it spits out and sucks in, that it neglects and retains? Categorics: to have loved and nothing more!

2

STEPS

for Paul Chanel Malenfant

The dance is wings, a matter of birds
and of departures into forever,
and of returns vibrant as arrows.
Stéphane Mallarmé

I With Each Leg, the Unforeseeable Swerve

The dance does not take steps to respond. Step by step. The dance is not a science of response, no more than the misstep that yet carries the day.

Above all, the action that really unfolds — as an occasion of happiness, for because of it, though not a response, the real becomes tolerable, tolerable to the point even of provoking desire for a response, of favouring the real with a richer countenance, deeper shadows, unheard-of angles, of favouring it with a Theory, however provisional, as to the real stakes put into play with each step, with each misstep that yet carries the day, with each tumble already slight and corrected by each leg each time reinvented under the body that falls, brutal and categoric — does not take steps to respond, step by step, is not a science of response.

The dance I imagine is not a matter of numbers or codes, related to god or faith or the son or a happy death; rather to the quick quiz and the unforeseeable swerve; for the dance I imagine certainly does not take steps to respond, for the dance I imagine is not a science of response.

2 The Dance Deals with the Adverbs

When suddenly the dance gives the adverbs a holiday. When there are only four memories which correspond to each re-created angle of the arm, the hip almost disjointed, the wing and the eyelash which fluttering signifies: "four memories in each corner when the head is in play" — then against boredom the dance suddenly gives the adverbs a holiday, steps out, closes up, beats with a cupped hand and a hollow sound steps out and closes up beats with a cupped hand and a hollow sound which resembles the cough of the monsters mornings with so much drink mornings with so much declamatory talk mornings with so much hope despite murder and madness.

When there are only four memories at each corner when the head is in play — for it will no longer be a question of death, much less the condition of the heart: to begin with there were the thick soups and the pepper, the vanilla ice-cream sodas, the well-groomed uncles then the mother who dances, giving the adverbs a holiday with each re-created angle of her arm, of her hip almost disjointed.

Other figures as well, but mornings, before the drink, before the hope, these are already quite enough for me to love.

3 Four Times Round to a Slow Tune

These are the things one says. These are the things one says. That the hand in a glove makes a fist, that a tireless series of steps might be called an "operation" — the front line and the chorus line — or "manoeuvres" — measures, exercises, large but dormant at times.

These are the things one says evenings of mourning and rejoicing, of mortaliy and fecundity, when the ankles, heavy and half asleep, turn on themselves four times round to a slow tune to a slow tune: in secret — agreed, I dance the secret dance best, I dance best in period dress, with at the end of each sleeve, in a glove, the hand that makes a fist, with the loud noises of fear and, with each leg, the tireless series of steps, precisely one by one, one by one, which one might call an "operation!", which one might call "manoeuvres!", one by one patiently in the way I would have it of each letter, of each note **à la carte,** in the way of each luminous point on the screen.

For these are the things one says, repeating in each case the gesture, the rhythm and the colours, beginning in each case again, one two and three, the serious play of signs.

4 The Body Falls More than It Gets Its Feet Flying

Fingernails even and lips and nose: a lexicon since, whether in grief or in showers, it's a question of arranging the world.

And as far as that's concerned the body has more expertise, as far as that's concerned it is less often a question of space, all things considered, than of gravity: for the body is always falling, more often than it gets its feet flying, the body falls much more often than it gets its feet flying, fingernails even, lips and nose, on drums or vocals (prose/opera), on drums or in song, in grief or in showers, it's a question of arranging the world.

Whoever watches, in secret, repeats, fingernails even and lips and nose start up all over again the body that falls much more often than it gets its feet flying: whoever watches, in secret, precisely repeats, minor, unverifiable almost, **in the dark,** repeats each time the body that dances, in the dark of the muscle, in the dark of the blood, each time the movement of the advance corps that dances, each time the lexicon of the advance corps that dances, since as far as that's concerned the body has more expertise, since, in grief or in showers, it's a question of arranging the world.

5 One Would Write: "Reality"

And moreover: were no one to vouch for it, nonetheless, and one more time, that would remain **the immediate test of the physical world.**

She says, then, "I no longer want to get hung up on being bitter." She says, then, "I no longer want to get hung up on being bitter, no more to blindly make a grab at beatitude." She says then, "I believe there's a purpose in things and sometimes that is enough." She stirs slowly, so that one can hardly say if it's gravity or the incredible lightness of being, when the leg, long and full, lifting and lowering, when the leg, long and full, falls or slips away from the hip almost disjointed, then, without insisting, lifts to here, indeed to here, to the point where with little hesitation one might write: "reality!"

It's the radical body that the movement, without magic, enlarges each time, the radical body that the movement enlarges: approval, acquiescence, not that her lucidity attenuates the joy, the radical body acquiesces to reality, wihout afterwards getting hung up on being bitter, without making a grab at beatitude, for there is a purpose in things and sometimes that is enough. She moves slowly, rises and dips, sinks or slides away, her hip playing supple and heavy, her hip singing supple or heavy: decidedly, **an immediate test of the physical world.**

6 Still Almost, She Danced

Zeno's arrow. Dante's boat. Never where you think it is.

Though hardly moving, her body is quick, and more. Seems finally to make no effort to move — from top to bottom — except to displace, imperceptibly at first, the strands of hair that fall, that give way to abandon, that she then gathers behind this ear of skin — one says "web"— between the thumb and the index (she speaks, she smiles at him, with one lip, she eats a little as well, with the other) — but that fall mostly and that mime undoing the flare as one says of the nostrils even to the angle, perfect, of the mouth that opens, mimes, and falls, "ah!" she says and this skin, web between the thumb and the index, of the right hand, gathers them there, again, there where they will never henceforth find the audacity to fall, will never more, despite the century, take up again the precise step of their flight: Zeno's arrow. Dante's boat.

He rises. He is going to leave her, tells her that. She has danced, for him, a last time, she has danced, sitting, still almost, in front of the meat, cold now, which she won't finish. Though hardly moving, her body has made itself quick, and more, the body has danced its grief, with this skin — "web" one says — between the thumb and the index. Then only, never there where one thinks, she moves away, her hair once more meticulously in place.

38

7 Last Movement

First movement: the body that drinks, that initiates once more the play of angles involved in drinking: the shoulder, frail at that, though one might think some violence was needed to put it out of place, the elbow, one might call it set, that one must nonetheless close up once more, a sharp angle then, to the lips and the wrist that turns, creaking almost so that each digit has beforehand the opening it needs for the body that drinks, that drinks, rests, that breathes, that initiates once more the play of angles involved in drinking.

Second movement: the body that dies, now at the angle of a table — in front of the plate, gone cold — now on the bench of summer where the painted wood bubbles and cracks in the heat, the body that dies a little in the manner of clum-sy sen-ten-ces **shall we dare say it** that dies, comes to an end, falls silent — before a cold plate, now — now on the bench of summer, where the painted wood bubbles, the green bench that dances and dies: elegant and modern.

Last movement: the body that's bluffing, dancing and bluffing, that plays its extremities, methodically, its tongue even when one expected nothing more from it, that plays its extremities because that's the way it is, that plays its extremities because the body that drinks, because the body that dies does not think of itself as a **centre,** has already vomited the **centre.** Last movement: undoubtedly because that's the way it is, the flesh is nomadic.

8 The First Step, at a Distance

Vertical, amid the furniture and the chests, also at times anxious about our carriage, our gait, airy and precarious or, at our feet, about the too slick tiles, we set out to explore continents. Vertical, we walk about; tall and unmoved, the body moves amid the furniture and the chests, head and thorax amid the furniture and the chests, bones and codes also at times anxious about its carriage, the chemistry of its walking: the small energies, the propellers, the sails and instruments, head and thorax — the body moves dances wanders.

The genre is traditionally tragic, every time the predictable itinerary that leads it, vociferous, from wicket to wicket, from corridor to interminable corridor, from cave, from cage, from grot, closed room to closed room; but, elegant in spite of the inevitable fall, it moves dances wanders amid the furniture and the chests, more, it insists: "I create nothing, I work at it, in stupefaction," it insists: "I create nothing, I start up all over again," more, there is nothing, even the word "body," more especially the French **"corps,"** that might make it doubt the exact nature of its trajectory — the guttural break-in and the infinite rolling or "R's." It creates nothing, it starts up all over again, anxious bones and anxious codes, the break-in and the infinite rolling.

As for the word "body," the word **"corps,"** it will find satisfaction, at the very moment of the first step, by placing the sense at a distance from the tongue, at a distance from its actual steps. Thus alone, amid the furniture and the chests, it moves dances wanders, in stupefaction finally.

9 Plato's Top

now the whole spindle has the same motion;
but, as the whole revolves in one
direction, the seven inner circles
move slowly in the other ...

Plato (Jowett, translator)

Zeno's arrow. Dante's boat. Plato's top — hooks, spindle, shaft and weights: **so interlinked one with another that in plane or in elevation they display the circumference of their ends.** Never there where one thinks.

This pack of reasons whereby thought stops the universe on its axis, this lack of reasons whereby thought, sliding away, ransacks the dry garden, dilapidates, though still, the very stones and redraws the map, this time with the living, their biographies, the adjectives (an excess of noise!) and the useless tremblings. For there are dances one can hardly imagine; that of the shade even more than its thick and balancing foliage, of the knot even more than the dexterous hands that untie it, of the final inertia of marbles already thrown more than the exact instance of their dispersion, which one can never repeat, and even more, the impetuous act, the arrest of the thigh, the sweet declinations of the siesta. Indeed, it is only the shade that explores, it is only the knot that explores.

Dances one can hardly imagine, so much they stall, so much they differ and defer — there still! — the first gesture, fearful beforehand of the type (hymen song or funeral march). Make do with this and that, make do with Plato's top. This lack of reasons whereby thought stops the universe on its axis, this pack of reasons whereby thought ransacks the dry garden.

IO I Danced Close to My Skeleton

"I lived close to my skeleton, almost tendered it an invitation when the tango was a must, taught it the whole sequence of steps, patiently pointed out to it the Drama involved, bending my neck and forcing, one by one, body and bent bow, the whole sequence of vertebrae, creaking, into perfect accord with the two-beat lamento. I lived close to my skeleton. My dancing was categorical."

He thought, however, that never again would it be a question of death, much less of the condition of the heart — the fragility of the veil or the thick blood — that in a higher sense, that in his "desire for the worst," the figures would become manifest, that therein he would master the meaningless: the predicate, the family, sometimes the shambles. For it is true that death does not conform, does not conform either as a type or as a series, is not grammatical — even when one takes care, now with the conjugation of tenses, now with the agreement of person and number — does not conform.

"I danced, then, beside myself, elsewhere, between two tempos — exactly! — of the lamento; and in harmony with this interminable, unimaginably slow tune, my body suddenly became still like a single muscle, long and pink — the fragility of the veil or the thick blood — whose underside one might have secretly glimpsed."

II The Body, We Have One

> the dance ... is a **delirious blank**
> **Pierre Legendre**

The body, we have one. We have one, a body that, in politic
fashion calling out the names of each of its parts — **piercing,**
when its desire still cries to the heavens — turns on its sex,
fabulous and agile. The body, we have one that resonates with
love: **assault and battery** and something else that one some-
times calls "thought" and sometimes plain "riot."

But what is it that dies, then, in each figure, if not the body's
other trying to seize itself with joy? The movement of the arm,
the movement of the long legs, almost razor-cut from the too
thin groin, the movement of the ankles, themselves dancers, of
the slight breasts, carefully kept in the clear, whose nipples are
nonetheless lifted in a smile, the movement finally of the hip,
itself astonished, reversed on its axis. What is it that dies in
each figure, if not the body's other, astride some Argentinian
tune? I do not speak of "mysteries," of "legends," of "utopian
arcana," I speak of "things of the body," I speak of "the body"
— I say, "the body, we have one!"

Carried to that extreme it cries out as a whole, it repeats itself
to death asking who would deny its claims? Carried to that
extreme, eternal and precarious, it is only when it stops that it
truly belongs to the world of speed, of movement, in politic
fashion calling out the names of each of its parts, calling out
its undying truth.

I2 In the Light Tapping of Slippered Feet

> the illegible bits mark the moments when, as the
> Japanese say, one detects the **ah!** of things
> **Alain Borer**

Two brief propositions for the four weeks of March: "It is
never just the Angel or just the Beast that falls"; "High and
low are merely **limit terms.**"

So the dance is also a way of reinventing the Fall, one two and
three, of Falling again, of looking for one's backsides: squint-
ing one's eyes, breaking one's neck next to the bone that
bends, sliding with each step on the secretions — buttery
odours! — it's daring the blood to bite into the quick as into
Italian rondures. Yes, indeed, a lovers' lexicon for the four
interminable weeks of March: passionately qualifying the fig-
ure, even its rules, the knee-movement where the knee has
been strained, the ankles or the hip almost disjointed, passion-
ately qualifying whatever **these apprehend of the real.**

"High and low are merely **limit terms**"; to be confounded
there in the light tapping of slippered feet.

I3 Her Airy Shoulder Blades Beneath the Camisole

there is a lightness we will never know
Philippe Sollers

An **impossible** case, in **that** corner of the world: a body lost to itself, wrested from us in **that** corner of the world, and that dances surreptitiously — rapt, apart, **last night!** — what the muscles search for, hesitant, in **that** corner of the world, for it is true that nothing exists that does not own to something, nothing penetrating that does not own to the docks whelmed by the sun in the east of the capitals, nothing with rhythm that does not own to the airy shoulder blades beneath the camisole, a body lost to itself — from the **male** insect, rapt, **last night!** — wrested from us in **that** corner of the world.

To see what one is going to see, for that reason: nothing springing up without owning to the reddish buds of the breasts beneath the camisole and the disturbing humidity under each knee as the leg, long and full, the shivers as the leg, long and full ... for that reason, the shivers: four syllables that dance surreptitiously.

Four, as one says, "an **impossible** case, in **that** corner of the world," four counter-images of the body lost to itself, given over to encumberments: the body in a lounge chair, the animal body, **another** body, the word "body," in jokes, in horoscopes, four counter-images, but a single dance: if you can, imagine the style of it, imagine one two and three each of these steps, in **that** corner of the world.

14 The Lively Fold of the Skirt

There is no imitation. Nothing, before. No more than, for that matter, tomorrow a new beauty, seized upon, to be again re-created. Only a rather insistent point that breaks into the scene, then the interval, reversed yet similar, of the sudden swerve or of being swept up into air; that's how it is: the point that digs in, swirling, and the lift, the elevation, the one adding to the other; nothing, before, there is no imitation, let alone comparison between the step and the emotion or indeed the thrust, the lift, toward some painfully unattainable ideal. Literally, only a body in a real space — no more than tomorrow a new beauty, seized upon, to be again re-created.

Plato's top. Zeno's arrow. Dante's boat. Quite different and yet the same, the lively fold of the skirt leaves no trace in its swirling except the double bind of the Idea and the Law. Besides it is now appropriate **to distinguish between two rehearsals, two performances:** "What is literature?" and "A dancer, alone, reinvents **the History of Meaning.**"

But there is no imitation. Nothing, before. No more than, for that matter, tomorrow a new beauty, seized upon, to be again re-created. Repeating without knowing: the book will henceforth try to suffice.

I5 Alone in a Pas de Deux

but who is the dancer, the first dancer, who has
just risen? I'm going to say, I'm going to focus
my thoughts on how the dance begins
Michel Serres

"Who is the dancer?" I am neither dancer, nor Celt, nor cadaver. I know nothing of a state of Plague. Alone in a **pas de deux**, awkward and mechanical, overwhelmed already trying to imagine how it begins, simply to imagine the first move, of the foot, for example, creaking almost on its axis, of the forearm breaking, with a disagreeable small noise, the wrist or the hip disjointed repeating ungainly the brief and noisy play of the shoulder; dancing is fleeing each time alone in a **pas de deux** against death, dancing, fleeing, neither Celt nor cadaver, mornings I can do nothing about the state of Plague.

For there are those these days who yawn after making love and it's true that their breath at those moments smacks of the sacrificial fire, thick and acrid. "Who is the dancer, before the sacrifice?"

A city as well, a city now after the murder, instead of this body, foot wrist shoulder and hip, instead of this body that dances, a city of a thousand angles whose name gets around, then bemoans the fact: a dance in Rome before the sacrifice.

I6 To Dance Is Unlikely

Six infinitives dealing with the flesh and the spirit (inscriptions, effacements, secret trafficking: the endless adventure of this suffering): alive, **to balance** their star, alive, **to magnify** their star and **to shed** a bit of light on those disasters of the flesh and the spirit, **to ream** one of the names for this **nostalgie de la limite** (the one that signifies: "whether in its perfect immobility or its giant rush, the body is always plunging ahead, is always in hot pursuit"), **to dance, to dance.**

Four more: **to imagine** an underground dance of the flesh and the spirit, a dance whose name would begin with **"there has been writing, but now it is space that is represented and realized, for one can no longer doubt it: there has been writing"**; the day when that no longer suffices, **to speak** of the prehistory of the flesh and the spirit, thus **to speak of it:** a prehistory of the flesh, then a prehistory of the spirit; **to dance** is always highly improbable!

To dance, intransitive verb, is but one of the possible distributions of the flesh and the spirit (counter-operation, the exact angle of the drift, its repeated affirmation: the endless adventure of this suffering). Alive, to balance their star, alive, to magnify their star, intransitive verb of the flesh and of the spirit.

I7 Amid Clearing and Gaiety

I say it without laughing, no one repeats himself less than I

I am not the father of this slit
Roger Laporte

Forever open. Testifying to this single wound. For clearly I am beyond all consolation, dreaming of a dance that **would not begin** with the first movement of the marking body, of a dance without predictability that would no longer be preoccupied with its own dodge and with the impossible precision of this sheering apart, this single wound: **play that is always other** that **would not begin** with the first movement of the marking body. I side with this delayed action, this breaking metaphor, breaking and unpredictable with each step, breaking and retaining only the tremor of any proposition about reality, I side with the counter-dance and its politics, I side with the counter-dance and there it is: you must pay the price!

A few pieces surviving from the catastrophe will perhaps suffice to disavow each of its images: this nudity — my steps within my steps — which pretends to be mine; the partner's swerving away, which is only — there is no suitable name for this dance — a more redoubtable form of proximity; and even the spiralling away for a moment a straight line, an inextricable straight line from the very first movement amid clearing and gaiety!

(What I'm talking about is not, word for word, a thing to be said, or else requiring a language of extraordinary precision — purification and cold celebration! — a language that, beyond all consolation, in order to dream of a dance without any predictability, would make possible two definitions: the Figure and the Truth!)

18 The Wild Dance of the Communion Girls

Quite simply perhaps it's up to me to determine the centre, the quiver of the centre, in counter-life the forever broken **axis** of bodies, to arm the centre, even as in the frail light of May the wild dance of the communion girls, naked and fair beneath their fine-woven veils: an imperative invocation of happiness even to the end of time.

And one **additional** figure: to lighten this time the centre — pure movement! pure exile! — like the angels ascending and descending, ascending and descending in a world without language. But what of the son, then, hidden behind the father, already driven crazy by what, in direct confrontation, the Other affirms, the son makes bull's-eyes of each wing, each bow, the frilly percale of each wing, each bow. Target practice: the annunciation of the angel in the frail light of May, the annunciation of evil and madness.

To determine the centre, to arm the centre, to lighten the centre of this syllable off in the very heart of its name, **catastrophe:** there it is, the true dance, complete abandon, flow, in counter-life the forever broken axis of bodies crying, naked and fair beneath their fine-woven veils: "C'est **la mer allée, la mer allée!**": "It's the sea gone off with the sun," Rimbaud's "Infinité."

19 The Late-Blooming Flowers and the Boulevards

It's speed rediscovered at last — the birds and the wind in the openness of the littoral — speed rediscovered with the force of a slap. Dante's boat. Zeno's arrow. Plato's top. The hair streams in the mouth, and she is alone crying to the sea of marvels and shadows, the late-blooming flowers and the boulevards, the overhand lob of the fountains, the high corn and tough stems equal to the birds and the wind, it's speed rediscovered in the openness of the littoral, but she is alone crying — **vocero! vocero!** — alone opening wide her arms and legs to star the beach with her absolute dance.

I see this body. I see in the centre of this body, exactly under its heart, dark and pleasing, a rare inscription of eternity, its exact cut in the manner I would wish of a cut-out dress in a children's book, dark and pleasing, rare in crying out alone to the sea.

Speed at last recovered, nearly a transparence, nearly a curve, the late-blooming flowers and the boulevards, the overhand lob of the fountains and the high corn, its tough stems equal to the birds and the wind.

20 One Two and Three

your mother dances and fakes the dance
don't look at the belly of your mother dancing
Paul Chanel Malenfant

The body that dies, **le corps,** has already vomited the **centre** — doesn't the word itself, in the throat, leave a break-in and an infinite rolling? Midnight nearly. One two and three. Midnight nearly, midnight coloured by alcohol, by your body which is quick though hardly moving, by this radical body that acquiesces to reality with every misstep that yet carries the day. For it's a question of arranging the world. Let's enumerate!

The immobile even, one two and three, which dances so ardently, so extravagantly, the airy figures of the child you were, fleeing alone each time in a **pas de deux** against death. The immobile even, with each leg, against the tireless series of steps of the child you were and that I would have loved. You remember: "High and low are merely **limit terms.**" Midnight nearly, coloured by alcohol. Enumerate, the high, the low, enumerate: four syllables that dance surreptitiously!

It is really only the knot that explores — do we know how to think about that, the knot, one two and three; do we know how to think about the spiral itself a moment straight line inextricable straight line? Categorical: the body, we have one!

3

BRUSHSTROKES

for André Lamarre

Painting is a true three.
Hubert Damisch

I Clearing Up the Entire World

I know it well enough. And yet, the painters of prehistoric times, they too at moments, on bad days, must have thought to themselves: "we are living fruitless lives." I know it well enough. But isn't that, to be blunt, an everyday tragedy?

Still, every image does its bit to clear up the entire world. Each new image, one two and three, far from adding to the repertoire of figures, reduces it rather, brings us each time a little closer to this end whose form it is up to us to imagine, obsolete already, denying in the very moment of its conception the speed of its own coming. That's why — up to this point — each image does its bit to clear up the entire world.

Imagine them all. Prepare, almost gaily, but without much patience, the whole catalogue. With arrows and an entire apparatus, files and charts, with unlikely colours and trick perspectives, falsifying even the angle of the eye, with reflecting cones and Dutch squares, the suspicious-looking ambassadors and the bust of Voltaire. Better still, rank them methodically in a series in the manner I would like to rank the blue and white schoolgirls kneeling, giggling and touching one another at prayer, in the manner of mathematical tables, lines and columns, notes one after the other, in the manner in which writing secretly inscribes names, surnames and given names. For it's true we live fruitless lives. Let's clear up the entire world in order to imagine what might be left of its form and its wild abandon.

2 Among So Many Other Images: Prendre la Mer

"Taking the sea" or "setting out to sea." What an innocent translation from the French, **la langue mère,** my mother tongue. I can't take it that way: **Je ne peux pas la prendre comme ça.** No, the longer I look at it the more it appears that **prendre la mer** must itself be taken at face value, literally, if not more mysteriously — if not according to the letter of the Law, according to the letter of the Other, which this riddling strangely renders (Theory of Networking!).

Prendre la mer by the bootstraps or like a sex in the mouth; besides, doesn't one already glimpse here, among so many other images, one especially that carries a whiff of mash, of the fermenting mother? It appears, looking at it, as if a kind of licence on the sea allowed the myth to be reinvented, henceforth urbane, with no need to mask its mute monsters, odourless, even though it is taken up again each time with the precise emotion of the archetypal tale. **Prendre la mer, resolutely,** in a stroke denying its depth, irrevocably turning the code back on itself (Theory of the Embrace!).

Henceforth everything happens as if the child, on feverish evenings, could run, could dance, all the way up to the high, marine bedroom, could silently slip inside, to wait, to touch, and to be taken up, each time, not according to the letter of the Law, but the letter of the Other, which this riddling strangely renders.

3 Always the Lungs and the Bronchial Tubes Beneath the Prints of the Dresses

No male in the Musée de Cluny,
no male and no heaven.
Michel Serres

Nothing could be less modern, and it's the same with desire, when one spends too long looking at the finished and naked body: nostalgia often, much more so than lust. And above all, now, before the finished and naked body, this conviction that there are lungs and bronchial tubes beneath the dresses, make-up at times beneath the grey, fur-lined shifts of former days.

Then, checking the canvas more closely, the animals with impossible organs, you reiterate: **"all of that in this mad fear of bees, all of that for sure in your passion for lamps trained on alphabets and notebooks, all of that, believe me, even in your most painful fantasies, Alain P., Socrates, Lascaux."**

There are, I admit, unbearable underthings, when it comes to the finished body, for even when naked it has its folds and its rings, even when naked its print marks, its broad lines of suffering and madness. Very often nostalgia, much more so than lust: for the fabrics, for the laces, for the short stockings, for the jewels and the brooches, but above all for the gestures that spring from the fingertips, unfasten — then it's the thumb and the index — from the hands that go down to the ankles, "moved" one might think, or fly up to the neck, cutting off the head for a moment, and finally stopping, arrested, this time definitively, taking everything back, the muscles almost and the skin, alone now with its folds and its rings, its print marks and its broad lines of suffering and madness. Nothing could be less modern, true enough, than desire, certain evenings spent feasting the eye.

4 Egyptian in the Strasbourg Museum

In the painting by Sebastian Stosskopf entitled **The Five Senses of Summer,** there are six peaches whose damp and tender bloom reinvents the fruit at a stroke. A woman, delicately — the stem between the thumb and the index — picks one, one only, thus upsetting, clearly, the composition, so that in this very instant one sees its disintegration. How though, in the same picture — where not only are there fabrics in loud colours, but also the broken string of a lute whose pegs and scroll alone are visible in the righthand corner — how can this woman open her eye to gaze straight ahead at some improbable horizon — her left eye — impossible, unreal and too complete — orb, iris, pupil — denying her perfect profile? Egyptian almost in the Strasbourg Museum.

Nature herself is at fault if we find ourselves unable to arrive at some absolute representation. Nature herself is at fault; indeterminate, Nature herself is at fault, without clear declension or certain duration, Nature herself is at fault. And this eye, unreal and too complete, denying the perfect profile, is but an illustrative anecdote, a striking example, a singular sign in the very midst of her improbable countenance.

Allegory was no doubt necessary; all that remains for us now is to proceed patiently with its detailed notation, cautiously checking its inventory.

5 What One Calls "Landscape"

Nature **adds**. Analogous, in that respect, to Nature which **adds**: perspectives varying with the neck, unpronounceable colours and patches of shade; in the end, to be banal, what one calls "landscape," what one calls "meadow," "garden," sometimes "where there are human corpses," "orchards" and even — in the blandness of tepid water on one's face — a rather miserable way of imagining "river" (the St. Lawrence, the Danube, the Nile) — in the way one might picture a whole orchestra on the basis of the agile forearm of the conductor.

The only **illusion** possible then will depend on each bit of **still life** from Nature, thickly pencilled, on the day before the End of the World. Maybe at last we'll see the lines that are painted there and equally those that are not, that will not be comparable: approximations, vagaries, unfurling of lines that are painted and even of those that are not, no real depth, no operation, no given, only Nature, without protocol, which **adds**: unknowable, mountain, road and grass, a fuzzy dawn, some season repeated yet once again, some season, analogous in that respect to Nature, without protocol, one two and three, which **adds**.

As for its Mystery, it's our patient business to compromise that, in the word by word accounting, in the precise deductions from its sum — verification, list, enumeration — in the most complete repertoire: the figures of Nature — extremities and involuted folds, what one calls "landscape," what one calls "meadow" — the rhythms of Nature — "garden" sometimes "where there are human corpses" — the sounds of Nature: soft and loud no doubt on that day, loud and soft in the vagaries and unfurlings; for that, surely, will not be comparable.

59

6 Grey Even Before the Green of the Basil

> Grey should help language to triumph.
> **Gilbert Lascault**
> **on Paillot de Montabert**

The **little bit** always bears a **likeness.** This time, on the side of the bit: clouds more than light, air or fire, and grey even before the green of the basil: animals and apparel as well; two lovely elbows even more than, higher, the eyes that calibrate their angle; the small fibres of the sheet if not their field, if not their harvest, above: a sketched-in moon, an improvised night, creaks from the clothesline, old crocks on the clothesline; travelling: fine new teeth, almost articulate, in their nylon toilet kits; and on the table, a maquette, archetypal: high windows, a rose in the western façade, pillars in the knave and even the leaves — acanthus — in the capitals. For the **little bit** always bears a **likeness,** one need only enumerate the bits. The **bit** is to the overall **census** as grey is in turn to the whole spectrum.

On the side of the **bit,** a body quickly secretes its thread, from the hand — at the end of the arm that one would think, it's amazing, is alone truly alive — scratches, rubs, and scores the canvas, but the glass as well, but the head as well from which it takes aim, finger by finger, the algebraic units required, finger by finger, the precisely crazy alphabet of the **bit:** clouds more than light, air or fire, and grey even before the green of the basil.

Viewed from the left, the **bit** is sometimes enough to reveal this likeness between the visible and the loved; there is nothing there to imagine any more than there is to recognize: only see there its growing inertia, see there its gravity, at rest.

7 The World's Last Painting!

An early infidelity: making out an **open razor** in the bent body of a peasant woman as the **Angelus** sounds. That is called "pain," that is also called "fascination." This body, henceforth marked, I will never forget that it tenders me the blade and the slit, that it reveals and conceals, slices and gapes under the linen. What is it one so much fears to spy under the heavy skirts of the gleaners? Some plaster on the anus or ointments against vaginal burning? Who knows, even perhaps, for some, a family resemblance in the brown folds of the star! Then, scissors in the eyes — that is called "pain," that is called "fascination" — beyond that, more violently, one can but lick the blade and the slit, can but hack up one's lungs in loud screams!

This whole fabric is killing! It's killing, this whole fabric! It's the way she is leaning. It's the way she is poised. Even though you can't see any pulleys or wings, wouldn't you say she is getting ready, in her headstrong lightness, to take flight? Then, incomprehensibly, her disturbing lightness compels us, dancing, to look up at the clouds — **oxen** and **giants** — to re-conceive the poles of the Earth.

An early infidelity: making out the **open razor**, making out a winged machine in the bent body of a peasant woman as the **Angelus** sounds. And that could well be the World's last painting!

8 These Images That Are a Sickness

There are images, some evenings, that make it difficult to get on; images that are a sickness; images that glow with the luminosity of bare knees: then one might think, trembling even at the thought, that a very youthful hand is delicately placed on our sex. There are images that are a sickness: so with obscene precision, a number of old and rusty nuts break through a broad surface whose colours are **passé**, whose colours are **shady**, scaling; a quite simple subject however where, all things considered, it might be no more than a question of stars and a few sea birds. There are images in which the signs, moving and celestial, make up an indefinable speech of love.

Others still where it's not just a question of the void that is uncertain, nor just a question of the whites that might always be compromised. For there are indeed images that glow with the luminosity of bare knees and, at each corner the angle required to work in the overweight angel, the angle required to calculate, with astonishing precision, the exact time of his fall, arrested.

With no magic, what's more with no "theory of clouds," there are, some evenings, images that make it difficult to get on; those most often that memory labels "pangs" or "awakening of wings," those whose voices, henceforth powerless to faithfully recall the occasion, are satisfied with repeating the title, over and over the title: one two and three, there are images that are a sickness.

9 The Theory of Green

"For a long time I believed the word 'raucous' meant a colour. Not, as the magic of sound might lead one to suppose, a particular and hesitant variation of rock grey and rufous, but rather, by an unexpected caprice of rhyme, of green — a green, as they say, that evokes the water of the sea. Also, for a number of years, that would have lent a meaning to certain organs and a bluish colour to several overly groomed uncles."

Does anybody know that there exist, depending on the light of the season, tones proper to the weeping flesh of humans? Behind each shutter, mysteriously, the angle of a single lattice, each time different, makes it possible to distinguish in the aperture all its nuances. The child especially is good at this, the one who, every evening, on his knees or elbows, on tiptoe even, reciting his catechism in a slow and hushed voice, picks out this slit and impassively observes it at length, then returns to his small bed where he already dreams of the oh so blue voices of his uncles. For there exist — how can one henceforth doubt it? — depending on the light of the season, tones proper to the weeping flesh of humans.

So, if it resonates infinitely, a single word will often suffice. Thus there are those who go on living, repeating it, there are those who go on, each night, with this simple word, right up to the moment of sleep, still on their lips. "Raucous" evoked a colour, a particular green that would recall — as they say — the water of the sea.

IO The Shoes of van Gogh and those of Magritte

Those things one risks in quiet caves, blowing them hard against the already slimy wall; those that are pointless beyond being nameless, simple deposits: make-up on the knuckles, which leaves a lovely trace — **all the matter of the century!** — those things that go on working, mournfully, and those that patiently wait for someone to attempt a simple description **("Certain things, it's amazing — do they not bear a resemblance to the words that one will never know how to pronounce properly? And besides, were one to do so just once, suddenly in every direction — even to their trace in memory — they would simply fade out.").**

Other things as well, against the wall in the children's bedrooms when they're filled with chatter; or enamelled and fervent in the acrid smoke of a fireplace; the shoes of van Gogh and those of Magritte; those with hard cores; those which suddenly open up to a castle in the Highlands of Scotland or a few spots against death **("But does one truly recognize, in each of these cases, the surgery on the body of the onlooker?").**

Those that quote; those that, theoretical, extend their decrees to the far corners of the planets, to the meaning of each line in the mirror; those that claim to save us from disorder and that are attached to skinny necks which in turn suddenly panic and hang themselves; with my every thought, immediately, the one that you are, equally the one that I am, in effect, by my mother **("And more still in the album, but for now that's enough. Let's clear up the entire world, let's then clear up the entire world in order to imagine what might be left of its form and its wild abandon.").**

II A Few Shallow Lines

The images from which one wakes so badly, distinctly crying out a woman's name, jaws sore from having held it back so much and blood gone sluggish before the first drink. These are **benighted** images, aggravating beyond belief the burden of the species, aggravating — between self and matter — beyond belief the agitation of the species; these are images that clutter, that's absolutely certain: images that clutter, before the first drink, astonishing in the morning.

Is it not intolerable that one should say "dream," that one should say "illusion," or "it's only ... it's only ...", is it not truly intolerable that one should say "dream" while trembling all day at the thought, repeating in a hushed voice a name unknown only a short time ago, jaws still sore from having held it back so much? These images, so **real**, so gently devastating, from which nothing remains by evening except a few shallow lines in the warm red polish of an old toy — forever, in the warm red polish, distinctly crying out.

And perhaps one will never recognize in all this, in all eternity, either the woman or the night; and of the name: we will no doubt retain only the rhyme, only the four **tender and sonorous** syllables, only the blood gone sluggish before the first drink, astonishing, in the morning. These images that it would be inappropriate to identify, to put a name on — besides, hasn't one repeated it enough already? — unpronounceable on waking, only a few shallow lines, DISTINCTLY CRYING OUT.

I2 The Severed Head of Iokanaan

> An ambiguous figure. One that is perfectly clear
> where yet it is said that the meaning is hidden.
> **Pascal**

In a prolonged hand to hand combat, convulsive in the space framed by the images, it's a matter of real willpower just to lift, veil after veil, one's gaze, to really take in what one sees on the platter — let's imagine a rehearsal without memory — the severed head of Iokanaan. It's a matter of real willpower to lift one's gaze to what is terrible and delicious.

For in the fullness of reality — is it not hollow, reality that unfolds at a stroke? — there is a streaming forth and it's very often only by means of a quite roundabout detour, absolutely the opposite of the silly sparkle of the vanishing point, that we are suddenly gripped by what one must seriously characterize as **the detailed imagination**: a deserted square, it's summer; some slim ankles and their light steps before the first wave; and in the glass panes, the precise colouring of the steamy air in the ward for the critically ill, and even the odours, yes, heavy and lingering, the same old adjectives (an excess of noise) succeed in evoking them; a deserted square, it's summer; happily here we are at war.

It's a matter of real willpower just to lift one's gaze at the end of an excessively long paragraph and to see, there on the wall, each shadow trembling, and immediately to recompose the landscape, there on the wall to recompose the landscape, with its greys, with its gaps, with the perfectly clear figure where yet **it is said the meaning is hidden.**

13 The Place of Heaven and of Earth

The primrose path and the forget-me-knot at the vanishing point, three episodes questioning once again the place of Heaven and of Earth: abridging (finding the calm at the centre of the storm); taking the measure of the sign, and taking the measure of the thing (in the end, will we find a single cloud in the instruments?); translating the field, the valley, each to its appropriate square, translating the oceans (an immense crossing, heat exchangers in the high windows rigorously trained on the islands) to the appropriate squares; three episodes where it's a question of the **view,** the form that is slowly filled out to define the **view: ev-en in-clud-ing the bar-bar-ic, a clear cat-e-gory, ver-tic-al right up to the deep-est black.**

"In the first light of dawn, tailored exactly to the rent in the heavens, we will perceive simple geometric forms: pale pink, for example, a woman's neck amidst scarves, fichus, then a few stars lined up not far from the angle the neck makes with the shoulder, and behind that, a single line — the word is precise — questioning still the place of Heaven and of Earth."

For ink and water sometimes translate the World: from the promise of fruit in the inchoate gurglings of an oar right up to the overall outline of a landscape; ink and water sometimes translate the World, what's already there of the World, which is sufficient for ink, which is sufficient for water.

14 Even the Eyelids Cast Shadows

Underarms peppery in the closeness of verandas. At this hour, in the smells of ether and damp tweed, even the eyelids cast shadows, lines, meadowy patches in gothic panels, all the way to the bench where, seated, you solemnly repeat in a hushed voice the name of the planet, you gaze at the summer dawn and repeat in a hushed voice the name of the planet — this time, it appears, you would like to be really convinced.

Underarms peppery in the closeness of verandas, we will later talk of this friend who put a bullet in his head and, trying to imagine the mark in his forehead, in November, we will hesitate between orchid and star; we will settle at last for something more ordinary in order to forget as quickly as possible this mark on his forehead and the bullet inside, in November, between orchid and star; we will turn instead to the question of these women who all write books and have the same first name, we will turn to something more pleasant, my arm resting ever so lightly on your shoulders.

People will see us from the back, in the closeness of verandas, will see us there, terrestrials, striding over nests and villages, repeating in a hushed voice the name of the planet.

I5 Against a Background of Diverse Figures

I speak alone, to a few, against a background of diverse figures. I speak alone, to a few. Whatever the sainted legend, always the first link takes on the sombre form of the death of a loved one — crudely, I think, one says "the remains" — and I imagine your smile as well, one day, before my own gumbo-like ashes. I speak alone, to a few; there are rare shapes, there are rare shapes in each individual desert, four millennia of intimate deserts against a background of diverse figures.

So, in the unsettled dark, does the Pharaoh not dream of cattle, and ears of corn, the school chaplain of the slight frames of his girls, kneeling, submissive, and the philosopher of the clinching argument to escape from History, for, he asserts: **"There's a hole in the whole system, in the strongest sense of a slap in the face, just think of the sea which one says is "high" even though it may disappear, each time more "low" than the horizon itself; the system embezzles, that's certain; reality is a joke, in the strongest sense of a slap in the face."**

I speak alone, to a few, since, despite pigments, varnish, grouts, there's no escaping the sentence; categorical, it rifles everything, even the rituals, even the lovely **frissons,** categorical, it installs its inner circles, its privileged pales, cosmologies of sentences in the heart of the city: there is no doubt about it, it is opacity itself, it is **the very currency and compass of disaster.**

16 Women Bathing and Self-Portraits

It seems to me one's got to be able to learn how to breathe in front of certain images, taking them like fresh salt on a canker, or better still like white wine rolled round on the tongue. Already it would be defending a form, it would be celebrating its exceptional nature — ideology, without the heaviness — for to go on doing watercolours of women bathing and self-portraits, that no longer requires there be a World!

I know why some things — one: organs, lots of organs; two: death, the figure, the fact; and three: the silhouetting of a Hebrew navigator — radically transform reality and reaffirm the extreme idiocy of poems. Some things — "**it's when it is least expected meaning storms us**" ... whence the comic, whence the dazzling effect, whence the rectangle and the ratchet in the throat trying to catch its breath. To be able to learn how to breathe in front of certain images, since after all a technique — that hardly requires there be a World! But let's wait until after the war, we will talk about it again, let's wait until after the war.

For now, is it not enough for us to recognize, however distractedly, something in the light of Sundays, a kind of suspended animation, a kind of wiping clean of the canvas (a painting finally that would be only a luminous vanishing point ...) and **the farthest reach** of writing? Defending a form: from the word go, to look at things from **that** level of vision.

17 The Cold of the Pre-War Years

and if I go on writing it's only because
the absence of any response forbids
even the certainty of despair
Roger Laporte

It's often a question of disrupting the shadows to the point of radiance, to the point of their taking on form and displaying its radiance, for form also is a defence against the cold of the pre-war years.

Gaining the time needed to live longer, to see all the images: I say one can laugh without transcendence, one can do something out of love without transcendence, disrupt the shadows and **pass through meaning** without transcendence, I say that however haunted by shadows — is this not the case with certain railway stations in Italy and a few ageing nostalgias? — reality is bearable.

For form too is a defence against the cold of the pre-war years and, sometimes, against the yellowish make-up that in the half-light of steamy cafés reveals more than it hides. It's called "gaining the time needed to see all the images": making things lighter, making each thing lighter to the point of tenderness, and **passing through meaning;** after all, it's only a defence against the cold of the pre-war years, it's only a way of disrupting the shadows to the point of radiance, to the point of their taking on form and displaying its radiance.

18 With All the Precision Required

This uncertainty above all, the powerful beauty of this uncertainty. As: does one, eventually, really discover how to take aim, with all the precision required, at a knot of scarves, a nest of wide ribbons? As: by endlessly repeating it, both the name and the thing, theory always appears to be as interminable as chastity. Sign and counter-sign. That's the gist of it. For often it's just a matter of finding a place in space. Sign and counter-sign. That's the gist of it. It happens one calls that the work of representation, but the point remains: the map one ends up conceiving is never in the end the precise map. Neither in science nor in narration. Sign and counter-sign may perhaps trace its borders. That's the gist of it. Happily, here we are at war, here we are in a state of Plague!

The language tells us: **"See here, you should never pronounce something dead whose resurrection, however slight, makes you fearful"**; the language tells us: **"It has even happened — and that before certain prophets proclaim its end — one calls that the work of representation!"**

Happily, here we are in a state of Plague and whoever, by dint of scrubbing the back of his century now carries it, finds his place in space, whoever carries it knows how to render, with all the precision required, the powerful beauty of its uncertainty.

19 This Prose, a Single Image

The wheat makes a great stir in the standing heat of summer. This is it, the authentic **touch of reality**: the wheat makes a great stir in the standing heat of summer. And just there, confronting this image, my own death must have begun. A child, first of all, puffing up his cheeks and blowing out frail strings of soap bubbles; later, in the arms of women, becoming one with the sea and with the nests of birds, a mountain bearing my name under an immense sky, a mountain with porticos, with bridges and porticos, a mountain with white spaces creating zones of silence, becoming one with the sea and the nests of birds, then only will I be pacified, for "the wheat makes a great stir in the standing heat of summer": a single image against my hatred of other-worlds.

A single image against the nightmare of History, everything happens as if a single image created, there in the garden, the nightmare of History: one very beautiful face wiped out behind its veil, sunny smile wiped out, sunny and without liturgical guile behind its veil, there it is, the authentic **touch of reality**. Everything happens as if, with each re-reading of this prose, a single image, the wheat the sea or the mountain, were enough to set off the trembling and the description of trembling.

As it is: my fears! One may see, then, my death has truly begun.

20 One Two and Three

And that could well be the World's last painting: taking the sea, **prendre la mer,** with the precise emotion of the archetypal tale. Midnight nearly. One two and three. Midnight nearly, midnight coloured by alcohol, midnight with its four millennia of intimate deserts ceaselessly repeating in a hushed voice the name of the planet, translating its oceans each to the appropriate square. There are those who have survived to midnight nearly, these simple words on their lips. Let's clear up the world!

The invisible even, one two and three, that glows so extravagantly, glows on the forehead of the child you were reciting in a hushed voice her catechism. The invisible even, this willpower to lift one's gaze to what is terrible and delicious, for there have always been lungs and bronchial tubes beneath the dresses of the child you were and that I would have loved. You remember: "Nature adds. Nature herself is at fault." Midnight nearly, coloured by alcohol. Let's clear up the world, let's clear up the entire world!

For form too is a defence against the cold of the pre-war years and the powerful beauty of your uncertainty: a painting finally that would be only a luminous vanishing point one two and three DISTINCTLY CRYING OUT, only the precisely crazy alphabet of the bit DISTINCTLY CRYING OUT. Categorical: there are images that are a sickness, a single image will henceforth suffice against my hatred of other-worlds!

Afterword

Normand de Bellefeuille was born in 1949, teaches at Maisonneuve College in Montreal, and has been associated with a more or less postmodern generation of writers publishing with Les Herbes Rouges and La Nouvelle Barre du Jour. His book of short stories, *Ce que disait Alice* (1989), won Le Prix Adrienne-Choquette. *Catégoriques*, which won the Grand Prix de la poésie presented by La Fondation des Forges in Trois Rivières (1986), culminates his exploration of the prose poem, the transformation of traditional "lyrics" into "categorics."

Rhyme and symmetrical stanzas are replaced by the elaborate repetition of words, phrases, whole sentences, producing a coherent suite of texts that might be called a love poem or a meditation on art, music, the dance (one two and three) — and writing (four!) — or a formal game, like composing a triptych, a major sonata, a new form of "long poem."

The writing is characterized, as well, by its pervasive intertextuality, its references to Bellefeuille's own earlier texts, e.g. *Dans la conversation et la diction des monstres* (1980), to his fellow writer Claude Beausoleil's *Une certaine fin de siècle*, to the songs of Liz Story, the music of Philip Glass, of John Cage, of Latin America and of grand opera, to the paintings of Lascaux, David, Millet, Magritte — to the French philosopher and historian Michel Serres, and, as the epigraphs indicate, writers, from Plato to Dante to Nietzsche, from Cioran to his québécois compatriot, Hughes Corriveau. It is this floating world of signs, of discourse, within which we live; it helps to generate the poem, at the edges of discourse; and yet it works to integrate in its net the immediate moments in an actual romance, moments of childhood, moments of everday experience that may be both banal and poignant.

Repetition, though not exact, that is the body's health, the rhythm of the heart, literally, as well as of the dance. Serres, in his book on Livy's book on the origins of Rome, suggests that the dance begins when the tremors of the sacrificial victim are said to be ill-received by the gods, with the result that actual murder is replaced by representation, the dancing of professional actors. Life and death. The world and its representation. The dance — of feet, of sounds, of images, of words — itself an act and a representation — becomes in Bellefeuille's text *un pas de deux* against death.

Bellefeuille's most recent series of love poems *Obscènes* (1992) continues that theme, but in a more laconic, perhaps more "categoric" style. He is on the point of publishing a narrative work interspersed with photos in the series "Écritures/Ratures" of Les Éditions du Noroit.

D.G. Jones' numerous translations of Quebec poets have appeared in *Ellipse* and in such volumes as Paul-Marie Lapointe's *The Fifth Season* (1985) and Gaston Miron's *The March to Love* (1986). Jones is also a critic and poet, author of *Balthazar and Other Poems* (1988) and, with the artist Lucie Lambert, *A Thousand Hooded Eyes* (1990). He teaches at l'Université de Sherbrooke, and lives in North Hatley, Quebec.

Editor for the Press: Frank Davey
Printed in Canada

Coach House Press
401 (rear) Huron Street
Toronto, ON
M5S 2G5